The Adventures of Scuba Jack
Copyright 2021 by Beth Costanzo
All rights reserved

One of the most fascinating sea creatures is the killer whale. Also called the **Orca,** the killer whale is a massive creature that you can find in many different regions of the world. If you are swimming or riding a boat next to the killer whale, you'll definitely want to be careful!

Many people just notice the killer whale's size and then move on to look at other animals. That said, there are plenty of interesting facts about the killer whale. Whether you are just seeing a killer whale for the first time or want to learn more about this amazing creature, you will find some fascinating facts below.

# Interesting Facts About Killer Whales

As most other people do, let's start by looking at the killer whale's body. Make killer whales tend to be 20 to 26 feet long and weigh around six tons. That is about 13,000 pounds! Female killer whales aren't much smaller. They are around 16 to 23 feet and weigh around three to four tons. That is about 6,000 to 9,000 pounds.

Besides the massive nature of the killer whale, you will immediately notice that they have a black and white color. If you see a killer whale in the wild or at an aquarium, you will notice that it has a black back, a white chest, and white sides. You will also notice that the killer whale has a white patch above and behind its eye. This distinctive black and white color is beautiful. If you happen to come across a killer whale in the wild, you will immediately know that it is a killer whale!

From size and makeup, let's now talk about where you can find killer whales in the wild. The good news? The killer whale makes its home in many different places. They are found in every single ocean and in most seas. Near the United States, for instance, you can spot killer whales off the coast of California, Washington, Oregon, and Alaska. There are also plenty of killer whales off the East Coast of the United States. These present great opportunities to see killer whales in their natural habitats. You may even see them leaping out of the water when it is swimming. When a killer whale does this, it is called porpoising.

You may be surprised to learn that killer whales are part of the dolphin family. The first one appeared around 11 million years ago. There are three to five different types of killer whales. The most well-known types are called resident, transient, and offshore killer whales. These different types of killer whales often don't interact with each other.

When swimming through the water, killer whales have great eyesight. This is true when they are both above and below the water. Along with this, killer whales have terrific hearing and a great sense of touch. All of these characteristics come in handy when they are looking for food.

Killer whales are basically at the top of the food chain. They do not have any natural predators, so they are called apex predators. Killer whales love to hunt in groups and hunt a wide variety of animals. Some of the animals that they like to eat include sea birds, sea turtles, herring, salmon, and more. Because killer whales are so big, they need to eat quite a lot of food!

Besides hunting for food, killer whales spend their time resting, socializing, and traveling. When they are swimming, killer whales are sometimes seen jumping out of the water or slapping their tails against the water. There are several different reasons why they may do this. For example, they may do this to communicate with each other or even play with each other. Killer whales have complex social bonds. They stick with social groups (called pods) throughout their lives.

Now, let's talk about one of the most important parts of a killer whale's life. That is having children. Female killer whales are most fertile when they are about 20 years old. This means that this is the best time when female killer whales can have babies. To begin the breeding process, males make sure that they are breeding with females from other pods. The pregnancy period itself is between 15 and 18 months.

After the baby is born, he or she nurses with their mother for about one year. Unfortunately, however, about 50% of baby killer whales die before they turn one year old. Because female killer whales only breed for about 25 years, they stop when they are 40 years old. This means that throughout their lives, female killer whales produce about four to six living babies.

While killer whales are thought to be dangerous in Western cultures, killer whales rarely attack humans. Many humans like to participate in whale watching, but boat traffic can harm killer whales' health. Killer whales are also a popular attraction at aquariums and aquatic theme parks, but many organizations argue that killer whales should not be in captivity. In other words, they argue that killer whales only belong in the wild.

# An Extremely Fascinating Creature

*The Adventures of Scuba Jack*

As you can see, the killer whale is one of the most fascinating creatures in our oceans. Its size is extremely intimidating. It is very difficult to find an animal that is bigger than the killer whale. But along with this, killer whales are intelligent and social creatures. Whether you are on a boat in Alaska or are simply visiting your local aquarium, I hope that you take the time to admire this amazing animal!

# TICK THAT COMES NEXT

# COUNT AND WRITE

# WORD SEARCH

Find and circle the words listed below.

| O | H | B | I | R | D | D | U | S | Y |
|---|---|---|---|---|---|---|---|---|---|
| T | E | V | C | A | S | J | R | X | R |
| K | U | D | M | W | C | R | A | O | X |
| D | W | R | O | Y | E | E | V | B | D |
| O | M | T | T | L | G | X | Y | F | D |
| W | R | U | M | L | P | C | M | O | X |
| H | W | C | P | C | E | H | H | U | E |
| A | G | N | A | T | M | E | I | L | A |
| L | V | O | C | E | A | N | P | N | D |
| E | T | V | S | S | A | L | M | O | N |

Turtle     Ocean     Bird     Orca

Whale     Salmon     Dolphin

# MAZE

Help the orca find the group of orcas

# CONNECT THE DOTS

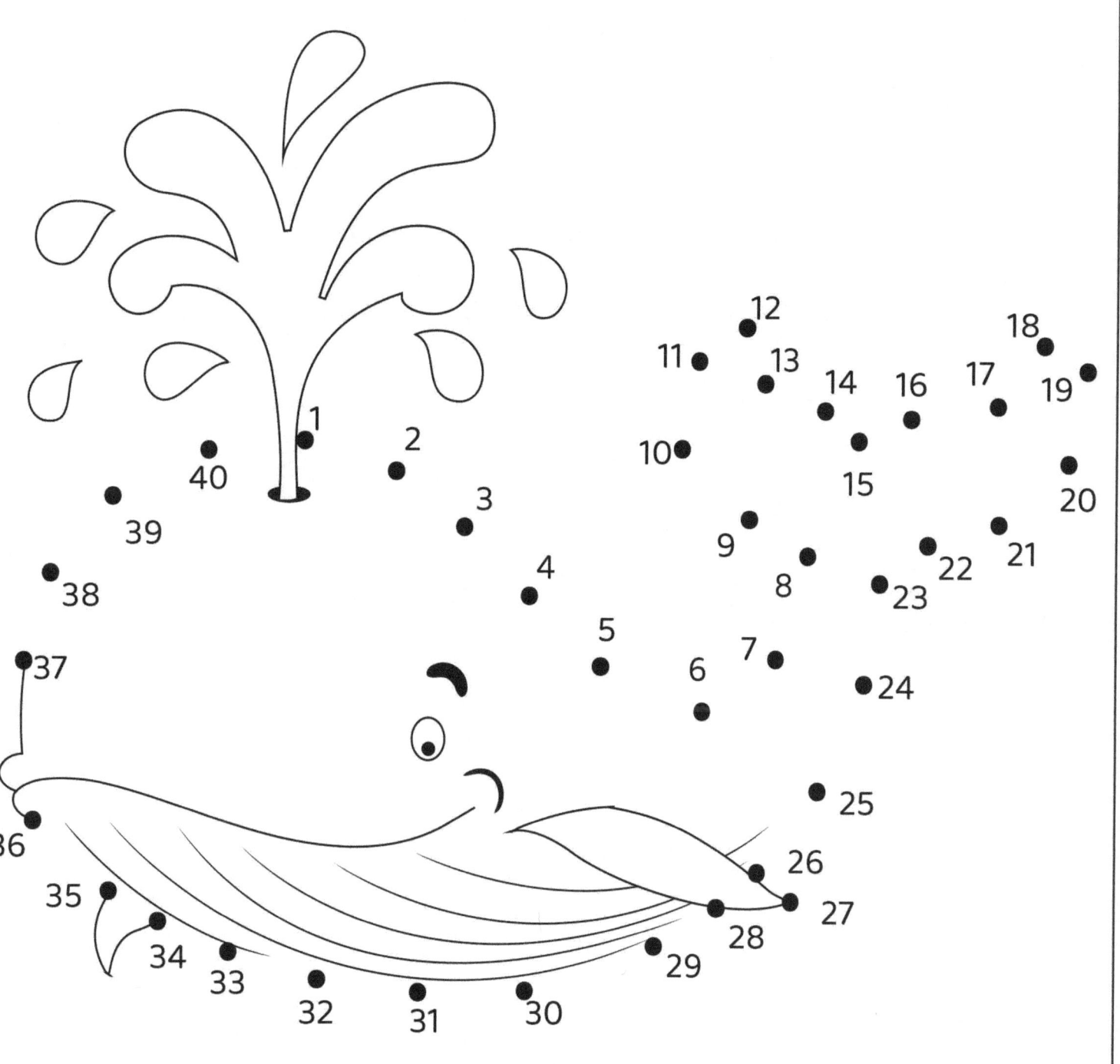

# DOT TO DOT

Link the dots then color the creature

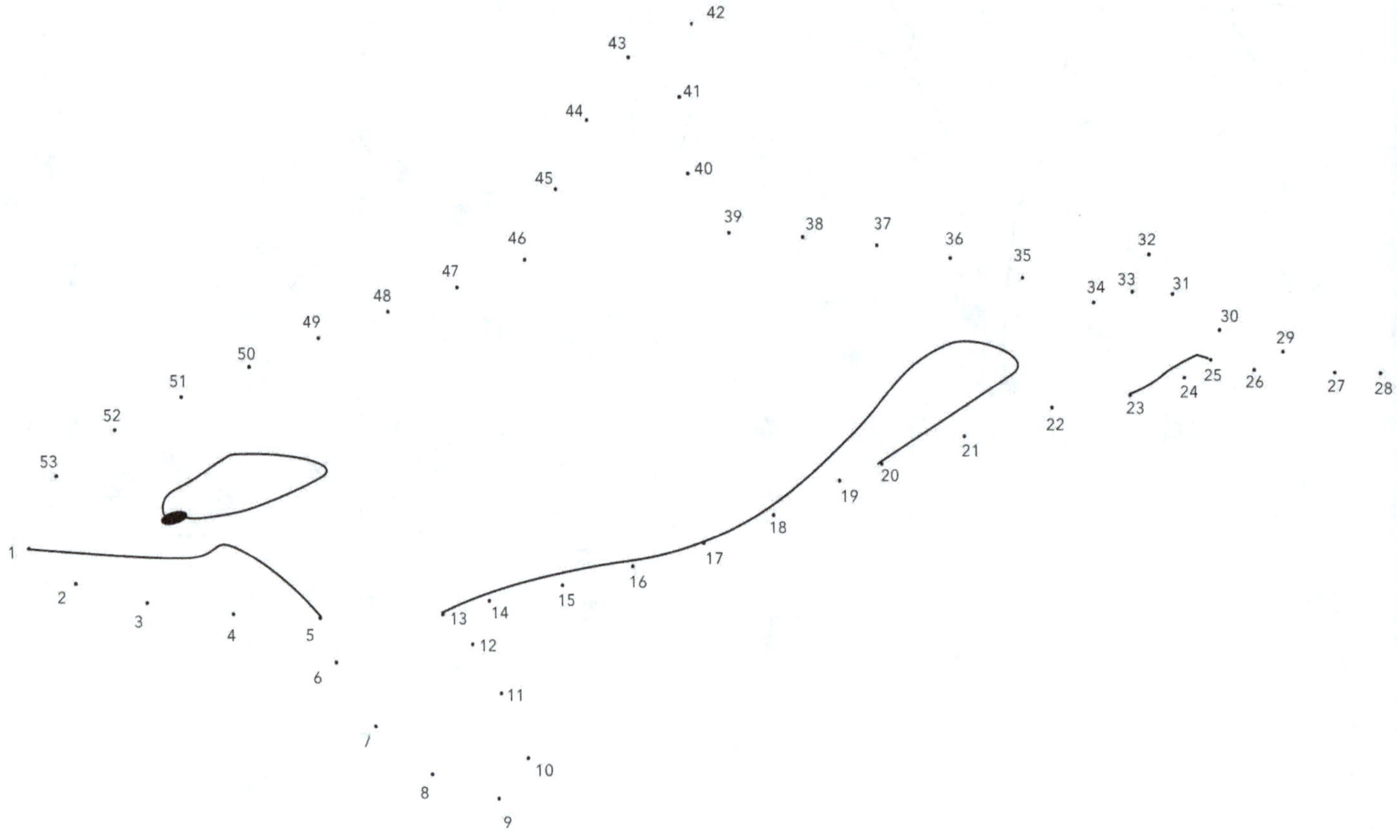


The Adventures of SCUBA JACK

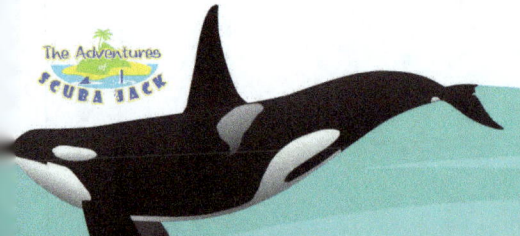

# COLORING

Color the artwork below

# COLOR IT!

# CRAFT

Glue the Orca's upper part to the bottom then add the eye.
Color the Orca.

Visit us at:

**www.adventuresofscubajack.com**

www.ingramcontent.com/pod-product-compliance
Lightning Source LLC
Chambersburg PA
CBHW060428010526
44118CB00017B/2411